You and Me

Let's Do It Together

Denise M. Jordan

Heinemann Library

Chicago, Illinois

Customer Service 888-454-2279
Visit our website at www.heinemannlibrary.com

Designed by Sue Emerson, Heinemann Library; Page layout by Que-Net Media™
Printed and bound in China by South China Printing Company Limited
Photo research by Janet Lankford Moran

08 07 06 05 04
10 9 8 7 6 5 4 3 2 1

Library of Congress Cataloging-in-Publication Data
Jordan, Denise.
    Let's do it together / Denise M. Jordan.
        p. cm. – (You and me)
Summary: Simple text and pictures explain when, where, why, and how we can help other people.
    ISBN 1-4034-4406-4 (HC), 1-4034-4412-9 (Pbk)
    1. Cooperativeness–Moral and ethical aspects–Juvenile literature.   2. Helping behavior–Juvenile literature.
[1. Cooperativeness. 2. Helpfulness.] I. Title.
    BJ1533.C74J67 2003
    177'.7–dc22

                                    2003012811

Acknowledgments
The author and publishers are grateful to the following for permission to reproduce copyright material:
pp. 4, 5, 16, 19 Myrleen Ferguson Cate/PhotoEdit Inc.; p. 6 Spencer Grant/PhotoEdit Inc.; pp. 7, 22, 24 Robert Lifson/ Heinemann Library; p. 8. Michael Keller/Corbis p. 9 Nancy Brown/Corbis; p. 10 Getty Images; p. 11 Corbis; pp. 12, 13, 14, 15 Que-Net/Heinemann Library; p. 17 Mary Kate Denny/PhotoEdit Inc.; p. 18 Ariel Skelley/Corbis; pp. 20, 21 Janet L. Moran/Oijoy Photography; p. 23 (T-B) Myrleen Ferguson Cate/PhotoEdit Inc., Myrleen Ferguson Cate/PhotoEdit Inc., Robert Lifson/Heinemann Library; back cover (L-R) Myrleen Ferguson Cate/PhotoEdit Inc., Que-Net/Heinemann Library

Cover photograph by Ariel Skelley/Corbis

Every effort has been made to contact copyright holders of any material reproduced in this book.
Any omissions will be rectified in subsequent printings if notice is given to the publisher.

Special thanks to our advisory panel for their help in the preparation of this book:

Alice Bethke, Library Consultant
Palo Alto, CA

Eileen Day, Preschool Teacher
Chicago, IL

Kathleen Gilbert,
Second Grade Teacher
Round Rock, TX

Sandra Gilbert,
Library Media Specialist
Fiest Elementary School
Houston, TX

Jan Gobeille,
Kindergarten Teacher
Garfield Elementary
Oakland, CA

Angela Leeper,
Educational Consultant
Wake Forest, NC

Some words are shown in bold, **like this.**
You can find them in the picture glossary on page 23.

Contents

What Is Helping?

Helping is doing something for or with someone else.

When you help someone, you **cooperate**.

Sometimes you work with others when you help.

Together, you can get a job done.

Where Can You Help?

You can help at home.

You can help at school.

You can help in your neighborhood, too.

You can help in many places.

Why Do You Help?

You help because it is a good thing to do.

You help because someone needs you to help them.

People working together can get a job done faster.

Helping makes a hard job easier.

Who Can You Help?

You can help your brother learn how to tie his shoes.

You can show him how to make a bow.

You can help your mom.

You can help her with the dishes after dinner.

What Do You See When You Help?

You see smiling faces when you help.

People are happy when you help them.

You can see a job getting done.

Jobs get done faster when people work together.

What Do You Hear When You Help?

You may hear "Thank you."

People say, "Thank you," after someone has helped them.

If someone tells you, "Thank you," you should say, "You are welcome."

Saying "You are welcome," is the polite thing to do.

How Can You Help at Home?

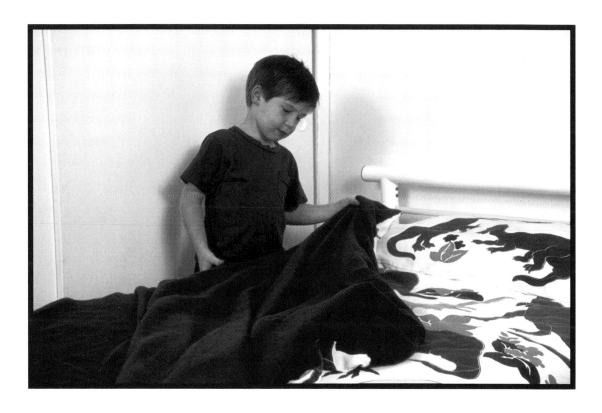

You can help with chores at home.

You can make your bed.

You can help set the table
for dinner.

You can give everyone a **napkin**.

How Can You Help in Your Neighborhood?

You can keep your neighborhood clean.

You can help rake leaves.

You can keep your neighborhood pretty.

You can help plant a **garden** with flowers.

How Do You Feel When You Help?

You can feel proud when you help others.

Helping others is a good thing to do.

You can make someone happy
when you help.

It feels good when you can make
someone else happy.

Quiz

How can you help?

Look for the answer on page 24.

Picture Glossary

 **cooperate**
page 4

 **garden**
page 19

 **napkin**
page 17

Note to Parents and Teachers

Reading for information is an important part of a child's literacy development. Learning begins with a question about something. Help children think of themselves as investigators and researchers by encouraging their questions about the world around them. Each chapter in this book begins with a question. Read the question together. Look at the pictures. Talk about what you think the answer might be. Then read the text to find out if your predictions were correct. Think of other questions you could ask about the topic, and discuss where you might find the answers.

Index

Answer to quiz on page 22

You can put the trash into a trash can.